THE NUTRIBULLET REC

70 Smoothie R

For

Weight Loss, Improved Health & ergy

By

No Nonsense Nosh

www.nononsensenosh.com

Contents

Introduction 8
Making a Smoothie 10
The Basics of Making a Smoothie 12
Top Tips for a Healthy Lifestyle 15
WEIGHT LOSS SMOOTHIES 17
Fire Me Up Ginger 18
Berry Seedy 20
Green Tea & Blueberry Smoothie 22
Grape Vitality 24
Mad For Melon 26
Red Hot Strawberries 28
Berry Pear Smoothie 29
Super Green Smoothie 30
Broccoli Blast 32
Sweet n' Green Smoothie 33
SUPERFOOD SMOOTHIES 35
Figgy Banana Smoothie 36
Brazilian Blast 38
Purple Power Blast 40
Nutty Blast 42
Blackberry Beauty 43
I Heart Acai 44
Apple Cherry Blast 46
Honey & Lemon Smoothie 48
Awesome Almond Smoothie 50
Berry Coconut Smoothie 52
SKIN BOOSTING SMOOTHIES 54

Clearly Cashew 56
Cleansing Cucumber 57
Sumptuous Strawberries 59
Beautiful Blueberry 61
Strawberry & Cashew 63
Strawberry Shine 65
Lemon & Mint 67
Sunflower Seed Smoothie 69
Awesome Almond Smoothie 70
Perfectly Pomegranate Smoothie 71
ENERGY BOOSTING & SPORTS SMOOTHIES 72
Peanut & Honey Blast 73
Beet It 74
Totally Bananas 76
Berry Nutty Smoothie 77
Kicking Kiwi 78
Wonderful Walnut Smoothie 79
The Energy Boost 80
Berry Boost 81
Chia & Mango Smoothie 82
BREAKFAST SMOOTHIES 83
Muesli & Banana Smoothie 84
Breakfast Boost 86
Strawberry & Banana Smoothie 87
Berry Breakfast 89
Peanut B Breakfast Smoothie 90
Strawberry Burst 91
Kindly Kiwi 92

Awakening Avocado 93
Mango Morning 94
Cinnamon Breakfast Smoothie 95
TREAT SWEET SMOOTHIES 96
Cheeky Chocolate Smoothie 97
Raspberry & Banana Smoothie 99
Tropical Treat 100
Perfectly Peach Smoothie 101
Mighty Mango Smoothie 102
Super Blueberries 103
Chocolate & Raspberry Pudding Smoothie 104
Zingy Ginger Smoothie 106
Kiwi & Orange Smoothie 108
Peachy Lemonade 109
GREEN SMOOTHIES 110
Go Green Go 111
The Avocado Smoothie 112
Pineapple & Kale Crunch 114
Green Apple Smoothie 115
Super Green Machine 117
Abundantly Green Smoothie 118
Apricot and Spinach Smoothie 120
Great Green Smoothie 121
Berry Avocado Smoothie 122
Broccoli Smoothie 123
THANKS FOR READING 125

DISCLAIMER

This book is not intended as a substitute for the medical advice of physicians. The reader should regularly consult a physician in matters relating to his/her health and particularly with respect to any symptoms that may require diagnosis or medical attention. Although the author and publisher have made every effort to ensure that the information in this book was correct at press time, the author and publisher do not assume and hereby disclaim any liability to any part for any loss, damage, or disruption caused by errors or omissions, whether such errors or omissions result from negligence, accident or any other cause.

This book has no affiliation with Homeland Housewares, LLC (the company that sells the NutriBullet™) and is intended as a supplement to the NutriBullet™. No Nonsense Nosh is not an authorised distributor of the trademark owner's products or services. This publication has not been approved or licensed by NutriBullet™ or Homeland Housewares LLC.

Introduction

We have owned our Nutribullet for just over a year. There are not many kitchen appliances that I can claim have been life changing, but the Nutribullet has been.

Since we bought our Nutribullet, it has been used almost every single day. It really has become a very versatile and dependable appliance in our kitchen.

As a family we like to try and ensure that we are consuming enough nutrients in our diet. However, despite our best intentions, this wasn't always happening on a daily basis. With busy work schedules and school life, creating healthy meals sometimes fell by the wayside.

Which is where daily smoothies have been a life changer for us. By using the Nutribullet we have been able to fill our bodies with a wide range of fruits, vegetables, nuts and seeds - all in a quick and easy to make drink.

Our health and general well-being has changed in ways I never thought possible;

- I have lost weight (through both smoothie cleanses and healthy eating)

- I am getting a much better night's sleep – in fact, I am sleeping less hours, yet the quality of my sleep has improved so much I don't feel tired.

- The need to reach for my nearest sugar rush has significantly diminished.

- My body is stronger – I enjoy running and by incorporating smoothies I have been able to run further and faster.
- The 'brain fog' has lifted. My concentration has improved enabling me to focus more when I am working – I am much more productive.

- The children are consuming so many more nutrients and vitamins – their sleep and behaviour has improved.

- My skin and hair looks healthy. My hairdresser commented on how smooth and shiny my hair has become recently – all that has changed is my smoothie routine. And most importantly;

I feel AMAZING

Making a Smoothie

You can make these smoothies in any high powered blender. However, the ones within this recipe book are aimed at the Nutribullet. This is for the simple reason that we have one and so have been able to test them out in this type of blender.

Using the Nutribullet for Smoothies

Using the Nutribullet is fairly straightforward, you can't really go far wrong. However, if you haven't used it before, it is worth familiarising yourself with some basics so that you can use it to its full potential. Please also refer to the manufacturer manual before your first use.

The Nutribullet is certainly a versatile blender and can be used for not only smoothies, but also soups, sauces and other meals.

Due to the high power of the Nutribullet you can put in and blend a wide variety of foods. Your smoothie will be exactly how it should be, free from lumps and lovely and smooth. All the essential nutrients will be extracted from the ingredients, ready for you to drink.

It is recommended by the manufacturer that you do not blend the following: apple seeds, apricot stones, cherry stones, plum stones, peach stones and avocado stones.

As a basic rule of thumb I tend to go with 40% fruit and 60% leafy greens with an optional boost of ground flax seed, nuts, seeds and sometimes a splash of honey.

I will then top it up with a liquid of my choice, never going above the MAX line. How much I put in, and what I put in, largely depends on what consistency I desire for that particular smoothie. Liquids I use include water, coconut water, green tea (chilled) and unsweetened nut milks.

If I have made a smoothie and the consistency is too thin for my liking I may add one of the following to thicken it up; half an avocado, ripe banana, Chia seeds or some oatmeal.

The Basics of Making a Smoothie

The Base Liquid

A liquid of some kind is required to aid in the blending of your ingredients, what you choose to add may depend on the other ingredients, or be a matter of preference.

Water is the easiest one to add, mainly because it is always available in the kitchen. Be careful how much water you add, do it little by little so you don't lose the taste of the smoothie.

Coconut water is a great liquid to use with your smoothie. Not only does it taste great and keep you hydrated, it is also full of healthy nutrients. Coconut water contains the five essential electrolytes found in the human body, potassium, calcium, magnesium, sodium and phosphorus. Coconut water is also very low in fat.

Green tea is rich in polyphenols and catechins that are said to be able to help fight various cancers and boost your heart health. Just make sure you allow it to cool first.

Unsweetened almond milk is a great source of vitamin E which contributes to the protection of cells from oxidative stress. Almond milk is 100% plant based and rich in antioxidants. It is also naturally low in fat and of course lactose free, making it easier to digest. It is also high in healthy fats, including omega fatty acids. It contains plenty of B vitamins including iron and riboflavin which are both very important for muscle healing and growth.

Fruits and Vegetables

The best ingredients that you can include in your smoothie are of the green and leafy kind. Top of the list is kale, spinach, watercress and romaine lettuce. The important thing with the greens is to try and rotate them and use different ones so you are getting an array of nutritional benefits.

Even if you don't think you like green leafy foods, start by putting in a little and gradually build up. Combined with the right ingredients, I promise you will barely know they are there!

As for other fruits and vegetables, pretty much anything goes, experiment with a wide range of colours to ensure you are getting a variety of vitamins.

Healthy Fats

Healthy fats will make you feel more energized and keep you feeling fuller for longer. I tend to use any of the following fats in my smoothies – avocados (so nutritious), nuts and seeds (packed full of fibre, protein, minerals, fat and vitamins), dark chocolate (try and choose an organic one high in cocoa content.)

Using Frozen Ingredients

It is perfectly fine to use frozen ingredients when making your smoothie. In fact, it is often beneficial as it means you can use certain fruits year round, plus, you can use them in place of ice cubes, smoothies always seem to taste nicer when they are ice cold.

If you are able to freeze any freshly bought ingredients this is a great way to make sure you always have some to hand. Chop it up and store it in freezer bags and containers.

When you are adding frozen fruit remember it will give the smoothie a thicker texture.

Ice Cubes

If I'm not using frozen ingredients I always put ice cubes in. How many you put in is up to you and how you like your smoothie. I usually add about 3 or 4 ice cubes but feel free to experiment to match your own preferences.

Sweetening it up

If you are used to sweeter tasting smoothies, it might take a little while for your taste buds to adjust. Feel free to add some sugar alternatives while you adjust. Just make sure you don't add refined sugar – the less processed a sugar is, the better. We will occasionally add one of the following to a smoothie – raw honey, dried fruits (dates, raisins or apricots) or maple syrup.

Added Extras

I will sometimes add some ground flax seed, spirulina or wheatgrass to my smoothie. All are available from good health stores or online.

Should You Buy Organic?

If you are able to buy it, organic food is always the better choice. As organic food is grown without pesticides, herbicides and fungicides, it is always the preferable option – but it isn't always feasible for whatever reason. If you are unable to buy organic just ensure you always remove the skins of citrus fruits, wash all berries and peel the skins from hard fruits and vegetables.

As a guideline, blend for about 30 seconds. Some recipes, depending on the ingredients, may require a little longer to be completely smooth.

Top Tips for a Healthy Lifestyle

As you are reading this book you must be committed to a healthier lifestyle. To ensure you really feel the difference from your smoothies, here are some tips to aid you in your new healthy lifestyle.

Go Natural

Eat as much unprocessed food as you possibly can. The more natural your food consumption, the better it is for your body and mind. Usually, once you are regularly incorporating healthy smoothies into your daily diet, your desires should naturally lean towards more natural foods.

Drink Water

Just because you are drinking healthy smoothies it doesn't mean you don't need to drink lots of water. Try to drink at least 8 glasses of water a day – not only will this help you stay hydrated, it will stop you thinking you are hungry when you're not. Drinking water will help to flush out all those toxins, keep your joints lubricated and your skin hydrated and younger looking. If you find drinking water boring, add a squeeze of lemon or lime to it.

Healthy Snacks

Probably my biggest downfall. I love to snack, usually through boredom and habit. There is nothing wrong with snacking, as long as you are putting the right kind in your mouth. Keep some raw carrots or cucumber with some hummus in the fridge. When you next open the fridge snack on that instead. Replace biscuits and crisps in the cupboard with seeds and nuts. Keep a fruit or nut snack in your bag when you go out, you are less likely to be tempted to reach for the nearest chocolate bar when you get a bit peckish.

Sleep

You may find your body naturally needs less sleep as you begin your smoothie journey. With all those added nutrients flowing through your body you will have much more energy. However, listen to your body and get enough sleep every night. Switch off the screens at least an hour before your usual bedtime so you can wind down and get a quality night's sleep.

Regular Exercise

Work your body often and you will see the benefits sooner. Try and do a variety of activities to keep it interesting. See if you can join any local clubs or find an exercise partner so you are less likely to slack off. Even just a regular 20 minute walk each day is a good starting point.

Take care of your body, it's the only place you have to live.

WEIGHT LOSS SMOOTHIES

Smoothies can help with your weight loss goals whether you want to lose a little or a lot. They can be used as a meal replacement or as part of a smoothie cleanse.

Just by incorporating some smoothies into your diet you should naturally feel like eating less sugary process foods and exercising more.

I find it helps to exchange one of my meals a day with a smoothie – breakfast usually works best for me, it sets me up in the right frame of mind for the rest of the day.

Prepare your weekly shopping list by thinking ahead what meals you will eat on each day. Clear your cupboards and fridge of crisps, biscuits and other items that are likely to jeopardise your weight loss goals.

Reward yourself when you have met some weight loss goals – perhaps a new item of clothing or a nice spa treatment.

Follow my healthy lifestyle tips in the previous chapter to help you too.

Fire Me Up Ginger

Ingredients

1 pear

1 medium carrot

1 apple

1tsp fresh root ginger

1 tablespoon of ground flaxseeds (optional)

Water

Ice cubes

Making It

Rinse all the ingredients. Chop the apple and pear, removing the seeds. Add all the ingredients to your blender, followed by the ice cubes and water.

Make sure the ingredients and water do not go past the MAX line. Twist on the Nutribullet blade and blend for about 20-30 seconds. Check the consistency and add more water if required before blending again.

Health Benefits

Apples and pears are high in dietary fibre and have a high water content. This aids weight loss by making you feel full up.

Carrots are naturally sweet and high in fibre and carotenoids. The high fibre content is great for weight management, making you feel fuller for longer.

Ginger plays an important role in weight loss by acting as a fat burner. Ginger excretes toxins from the body as well as acting as a natural appetite suppressant - this is great for weight loss, making you less likely to overindulge. Ginger is also well known for its incredible health benefits. It is full of nutrients that are very beneficial for your body and brain, with powerful antioxidant and anti-inflammatory benefits.

Love yourself enough to have a healthy lifestyle.

Berry Seedy

Ingredients

1 handful of spinach

1 medium ripe banana

100g frozen or fresh strawberries

Water

2 tbsps of Chia Seeds

Ice cubes

Making It

Rinse the strawberries (if using fresh) and spinach. Add all the ingredients to the Nutribullet cup followed by the ice cubes (if required) and the water (up to the MAX line).

Make sure the ingredients do not go past the MAX line. Twist on the Nutribullet blade and blend for about 20-30 seconds or until smooth.

Check the consistency and add more water if required before blending again.

Health Benefits

When people are trying to lose weight they often avoid foods they believe to be high in calories. A medium **banana** comes in at around 100 calories, which, when compared with some sweeter alternatives (such as biscuits, crisps etc) isn't that bad, and of course, bananas are full of healthy calories rather than the 'empty' calories of processed foods. Bananas are filling and sweet in taste, helping to curb any of those persistent sugar cravings.

Strawberries are another great addition for those who prefer sweet tasting foods. Strawberries speed up your metabolic rate by promoting the production of certain fat burning hormones.

Strawberries are also high in fibre which can be found in both the flesh of the fruit as well as the seeds. High fibred fruits not only help with making you feel fuller, they also assist with your digestive tract. This combined with their high water can help those who suffer from constipation.

Chia Seeds are rich in healthy omega-2 fatty acids, antioxidants, fibre, protein and a variety of micro nutrients. Aside from all these incredible health benefits, chia seeds also expand in size when you put them in liquid. Therefore, if you drink your smoothie shortly after making it, the seeds will expand in your stomach, making you feel full up. Chia seeds are 40% fibre by weight which makes them an incredible source of fibre.

"The groundwork of all happiness is health."
James Leigh Hunt

Green Tea & Blueberry Smoothie

Ingredients

1 handful of fresh or frozen blueberries

1 banana

1tsp of cinnamon

200ml chilled green tea

Ice cubes (if using fresh blueberries)

Making It

Make up 200ml of green tea and allow it to chill.

Rinse the blueberries (if using fresh). Pour the green tea into your Nutribullet blender followed by the remaining ingredients.

Make sure the ingredients do not go past the MAX line. Twist on the Nutribullet blade and blend for about 20-30 seconds or until smooth.

Check the consistency and add some water if required before blending again.

Health Benefits

Green tea makes a great alternative as a base for smoothies, it not only has the benefit of boosting metabolism, it is also thought to reduce bad cholesterol as well as being low in calories.

Cinnamon leaves you feeling fuller for longer and keeps blood sugar levels more balanced.

Blueberries are low in calories and contain no fat. They are full of powerful antioxidants, vitamin C and potassium. Blueberries are great for your digestive system due to the insoluble fibre they contain.

"To keep the body in good health is a duty, otherwise we shall not be able to keep our mind strong and clear."

Buddha

Grape Vitality

Ingredients

1 handful of romaine lettuce

1 medium carrot

2 handfuls of seedless grapes (green or red)

1 table spoon of ground flaxseed

Water

Ice cubes

Making It

If you want to you can freeze your grapes and take them out of the freezer as and when you require. Add all the ingredients to the Nutribullet cup followed by the water and ice cubes. Make sure you do not go past the MAX line.

Twist on the Nutribullet blade and blend for about 20-30 seconds or until smooth. Check the consistency and add more water if required before blending again.

Health Benefits

Grapes are a great source of vitamin B1. Vitamin B1 is great for providing your body with a great energy boost. They are low in calories and high in fibre. Plus, they taste great!

Romaine Lettuce has the highest nutritional benefits out of all lettuces. It has almost no fat and is incredibly low in calories (about 15 calories per shredded cup). Romaine lettuce also contains vitamin C and beta-carotene which is good for maintaining a healthy heart. Romaine lettuce also contains omega-3 and omega-6 essential fatty acids – but you would have to consume a lot of it to really notice the difference as the fat content is so low. It is also rich in iron and B-vitamins.

Ground Flaxseed contain many healthy fats and have a high fibre content. Flaxseed contains a plant-based omega-3 fatty acid (linolenic acid) that helps to increase the feelings of being full.

Mad For Melon

Ingredients

120g watermelon (about 2 cups)

100g of fresh or frozen strawberries (about 1 cup)

1 lemon (unwaxed if possible)

Water

Ice cubes (if not using frozen ingredients)

Making It

You won't need to include as much water in this recipe due to the high water content found in watermelons. Place all the ingredients in the Nutribullet followed by some water (just add a little at first and check the taste and consistency before you add any more). This is a smoothie perfect for hot summer days. Blend for 20 to 30 seconds and check the consistency. Add more water if needed.

Health Benefits

Watermelons don't contain quite as many nutrients as other fruits but they are high in beta-carotene and vitamin c. The beta-carotene found in watermelons converts into vitamin A in the body which is great for eye, skin and teeth health. They also contain lycopene (the same nutrient found in tomatoes). The high water content in watermelons make them a great ingredient to include in a smoothie to sip on to rehydrate during and after a workout, or throughout the day to keep yourself hydrated and skin looking clear.

Lemons are always a welcome nutritional boost to any drink or meal. Lemons contain vitamin C, fibre, calcium, vitamin B6 and potassium. They are also low in fat and cholesterol. The vitamin C content is a great immune booster as well as a remedy for coughs and colds.

"A healthy body is a guest-chamber for the soul; a sick body is a prison."

Francis Bacon

Red Hot Strawberries

Ingredients

100g of fresh or frozen strawberries (about 1 cup)

1/2 red chilli pepper

1 tsp of grated fresh root ginger

Juice of 2 oranges

Juice of half a lime

Water

Ice cubes

Making It

This is quite a unique taste for a smoothie and one that you perhaps might take some getting used to! Carefully slice the chilli and remove the seeds. If you are concerned you won't like the chilli factor then start with a smaller bit and add according to your taste.

Put all the ingredients in the Nutribullet cup and add some water and the ice cubes, remembering not to go above the MAX line.

Blend for about 20 to 30 seconds or until smooth. Add more water if required.

Health Benefits

Chilli Peppers have a compound in them called capsaicin which increases energy, suppresses your appetite and boosts metabolism. Chillis also raise your endorphin levels, making you feel great!

It isn't a diet, it's a lifestyle.

Berry Pear Smoothie

Ingredients

1 handful of spinach

1 handful of frozen or fresh mixed berries

2 pears, chopped with the skin still on.

Water

Ice Cubes (unless you are using frozen berries)

Making It

Wash the ingredients. Chop and core the pears. Add all the ingredients to the Nutribullet blender. Add some water and the ice cubes (if using). Do not fill above the MAX line.

Blend for about 20 to 30 seconds. Add more water if required.

Health Benefits

Pears are very fibrous so are very helpful for assisting with weight loss whilst still supplying important antioxidants and flavonoids. The skin of a pear contains about half of the pear's whole dietary fibre. The skin also contains many of the antioxidants of the pear.

Berries are also a great source of fibre, alongside other health benefits. For example, raspberries contain ketones which are said to prevent an increase in overall body fat. More importantly, berries taste fantastic and can really sweeten up a smoothie.

Spinach is high in antioxidants, vitamins A, K, B and C. Spinach is low in calories but incredibly rich in nutrients, making them the perfect addition to a weight loss smoothie.

You don't have to eat less, you just have to eat well.

Super Green Smoothie

Ingredients

1 handful of romaine lettuce

1 apple

1/2 ripe avocado

Half a lime

1 tsp of honey (Manuka if possible)

Water

Ice cubes

Making It

Wash the lettuce and apple. Chop the apple up removing the seeds. Scoop the avocado flesh from the skin. Peel the skin from the lime and chop in half.

Add all the ingredients to the Nutribullet cup adding some water and ice cubes. Make sure you don't go over the MAX line. Blend for about 20 to 30 seconds. Check the consistency and add more water if required.

Health Benefits

Avocado is one of the healthiest foods in the world. They ensure a balanced and nutritious diet. They are a brilliant source of fibre and are high in healthy fats. They are packed full of the 6 requirements for a healthy body; vitamins, minerals, protein, fat, water and natural sugar. They are high in vitamin E, potassium and iron.

The Lutein found in avocadoes is fantastic for good eye health, acting as an antioxidant to protect your eyes against age related issues.

Although the avocado is high in fat, it is monounsaturated fatty acid which translates into slow burning energy, rather than turning to body fat.

Apples are made up of mainly water (about 85%). Pectin is also found in apples, a soluble fibre which helps keep the digestive track healthy and regular.

Broccoli Blast

Ingredients

2 broccoli florets

1 apple

1 carrot

1 handful of fresh or frozen strawberries (about 100g)

Water

Ice cubes (if you are not using frozen fruit)

Making It

Wash the ingredients and chop the apple (removing the seeds) and carrot. Add all the ingredients to the Nutribullet blender adding the water and ice cubes (if required). Do not fill above the MAX line. Blend for about 20 to 30 seconds or until smooth. Add more water if required.

Health Benefits

Broccoli is a fantastic vegetable to include in your diet on a regular basis. Not only does it have almost as much calcium as milk, it also has twice as much protein as steak! It is packed full of antibacterial and antiviral nutrients.

Broccoli is also a great source of beta-carotene, calcium, vitamin C, potassium, magnesium and the vitamin B's. It is full of dietary fibres which is great for making you feel full up and creating longer lasting energy.

Create healthy habits.

Sweet n' Green Smoothie

Ingredients

1 handful of spinach

1 pear (ripe ones will be sweeter)

15-20 seedless grapes (red or green)

150ml fat free Greek yoghurt (plain)

Half a ripe avocado

Half a lemon (non-waxed)

Ice cubes

Making It

Wash the ingredients, chop and core the pear. Scoop out the flesh of half the avocado. Add all the ingredients to the Nutribullet blender including the ice cubes. Do not fill above the MAX line. Blend for about 20 to 30 seconds or until smooth. If required, add some water for a thinner consistency.

Health Benefits

Even a small amount of **Greek yoghurt** can pack a powerful punch when it comes to boosting your health. Greek yoghurt is a protein rich food, essential for your body's growth and repair. There are high levels of probiotics found in Greek yoghurt which contain beneficial bacteria such as lactobacillus. This friendly bacteria can help your gut maintain a healthy balance of bacteria and in turn, help your digestive system to stay healthy.

However, one of the star minerals when it comes to weight loss, is the high content of iodine found within Greek yoghurt. Iodine helps to control your body's metabolic rate by creating thyroid hormones. This can really aid with speeding up your calorie burn rate. What's more, iodine is a great energy booster, meaning you can work out more!

The only bad workout is the one that didn't happen.

SUPERFOOD SMOOTHIES

There always seems to be a latest 'superfood' being praised as the next can't live without food. So what makes an ingredient a superfood? Well, actually there is no legal or medical definition.

Green leafy plant food such as kale, spinach and watercress all make it on the list, but so do other non-plant based products such as salmon and sardines.

What they do tend to have in common though is that they all;

- Are rich in nutrients
- Contain health benefits to combat certain ailments
- Help reduce your risk of getting certain ailments

Love yourself. Love your body. Love your life.

Figgy Banana Smoothie

Ingredients

2 to 3 dried figs

2 small ripe bananas

2 tsp honey (Manuka if possible)

200ml almond milk (or a preferred alternative such as soya or rice)

Ice cubes

Making It

Add all the ingredients to the Nutribullet blender. Add the ice cubes and almond milk, making sure not to go above the MAX line. Blend for about 20 to 30 seconds. Check the consistency and add more almond milk if required (or a liquid of your choice).

Health Benefits

Figs are a naturally sweet fruit which can help with weight loss owing to their high fibre content, making you feel satisfied for longer. Figs can help with your digestive health due to the presence of prebiotics they contain, this helps assist the good bacteria already present in your gut. Figs are also a good source of nourishment due to their high calcium and potassium content.

Manuka Honey is one of the most expensive honeys on the market. It is native to bees on New Zealand's North Island who get the pollen from just one kind of flower only in bloom for 2 to 6 weeks of the year. When deciding which Manuka honey to buy, check out the UMF number on each jar. UMF stands for Unique Manuka Factor and grades the anti-bacterial potency level for each type. Try to go for something from 10+ upwards.

You have likely heard or read about the many benefits of Manuka honey. If you have a sweet craving, adding honey to your smoothie will help to curb that desire. Make sure you limit your daily intake to no more than about 3-4 tsps. Manuka can also help when taken internally with coughs, colds and digestive problems.

Externally, Manuka honey is said to help with skin conditions including acne, dry skin and wounds.

"Life is not merely to be alive, but to be well."

Marcus Valerius Martial

Brazilian Blast

Ingredients

1 apple

1 banana

1 handful of fresh or frozen mango

3 Brazil nuts

1 tbsp ground flax seeds

250ml coconut water or plain water

Ice cubes

Making It

Wash and chop the apple, removing the seeds. Add all the ingredients to the Nutribullet blender cup. Add the coconut water (or plain water) and the ice cubes taking care not to go over the MAX line.

Blend for about 20 to 30 seconds or until smooth. Check the consistency and add more water/coconut water if required.

Health Benefits

Brazil nuts are packed full of nutrients. They have an abundance of vitamins, antioxidants and minerals. One important antioxidant mineral that the Brazil nut has a lot of is selenium. Selenium helps maintain the elasticity and firmness of your skin. It can also help reduce sun damage.

Coconut water is a great alternative to sugary drinks and a healthy option to drink if you want to replace your usual soft or fizzy drink. It is cholesterol free, low in carbohydrates and 99% fat free. Although sugar is present in coconut water, it is naturally occurring.

Mangoes are a very popular fruit the world over. The delicious sweet taste is perfect for this tropical tasting smoothie. Mangoes are a fantastic source of vitamin A, C and B6. They are also high in dietary fibre and rich in potassium, magnesium and potassium. They are low in saturated fat, sodium and cholesterol.

The high vitamin A & C content makes mangoes an excellent anti-aging fruit. The high beta-carotene content is brilliant for your immune system and healthy eyes. Mangoes are also rich in iron, which is great for anaemia sufferers.

Who knew something so tasty would be so good for you?!

Don't eat anything incapable of rotting.

Purple Power Blast

Ingredients

2 handfuls of frozen/fresh mixed berries

1/2 tsp ground cinnamon

200ml pomegranate juice

50ml of probiotic vanilla yoghurt

Ice cubes (if you are not using frozen berries)

Making It

Add all the ingredients to the Nutribullet blender cup. Add the pomegranate juice and the ice cubes taking care not to go over the MAX line.

Blend for about 20 to 30 seconds or until smooth. Check the consistency and add more pomegranate juice/water if required.

Health Benefits

Berries are packed full of antioxidants, protecting your body and cells against inflammation. They are said to be helpful with easing the symptoms of arthritis.

Pomegranate and in particular, pomegranate juice, has remarkable levels of antioxidant properties. Pomegranates are abundantly rich in potassium, fibre, vitamin C, niacin and disease fighting antioxidants.

Cinnamon helps to balance blood sugar levels – and it also tastes just like Christmas!

Probiotic yoghurt contains good bacteria which is beneficial for the digestive system.

Hungry? That's ok, eat something healthy, your body needs fuel.

Nutty Blast

Ingredients

1 handful spinach

Walnuts (about 10)

1 banana

250ml of coconut water or plain water

Ice cubes

Making It

Wash the spinach and add all the ingredients to the Nutribullet blender. Add the coconut water or plain water with the ice cubes taking care not to go over the MAX line.

Blend for about 20 to 30 seconds or until smooth. Check the consistency and add more liquid if required.

Health Benefits

Walnuts are a brilliant source of fibre, protein and omega-3 fatty acids. It is good to include a variety of nuts in your diet if you can, but walnuts have the highest overall antioxidant properties of them all.

Spinach has powerful anti-ageing properties as well as containing eye health benefits. Spinach is rich in antioxidants including beta-carotene. It also has high levels of iron, so great for anaemia sufferers.

Food is fuel.

Blackberry Beauty

Ingredients

2 medium carrots

1 handful of fresh or frozen blackberries

2 kiwis

Half a lemon (unwaxed)

Water

Ice cubes

Making It

Wash and chop the carrots, peel the kiwis, wash the lemon (keep it's skin on if using unwaxed) and add everything to the blender. Add the water and ice cubes making sure you don't go over the MAX line.

Blend for about 20 to 30 seconds or until smooth. Check the consistency and add more water if required.

Health Benefits

Kiwis are a very nutrient rich fruit containing vitamins C, E and beta-carotene. They are full of healthy minerals including calcium, magnesium, phosphorus, potassium and sodium. They are great for providing you with an energy boost to start the day. The high vitamin C content will help strengthen your immune system too.

Blackberries are high in antioxidants, nutrients and fibre. They are virtually fat free and low in calories. The folic acid, vitamin K and C are all great for your joints and bones.

I don't chase rainbows, I eat them.

I Heart Acai

Ingredients

1 handful of spinach

1 tbsp of acai berries (fresh, dried or powdered)

1 handful of fresh or frozen blueberries

200ml of unsweetened nut milk or soy milk

Ice cubes (if you are not using frozen fruits)

Making It

Wash the spinach and berries (if using fresh) and put in the Nutribullet blender cup. Add the nut or soy milk and ice cubes. Blend for about 20 to 30 seconds or until smooth. If you require a thinner consistency add more nut/soy milk or water and blend again.

Health Benefits

Acai berries are native to Central and South America. Studies have shown that acai berries are very high in antioxidants and are said to help prevent blood clots by improving overall blood circulation and relaxing the blood vessels.

Soy milk is rich in omega 3 fatty acids, protein and is a great dairy alternative. Soy milk is good for keeping your cholesterol levels in check.

Blueberries are a very tasty addition to any smoothie, they are also a very healthy ingredient to include. Many nutritionists consider blueberries to be a superfood owing to their rich levels of antioxidants. Blueberries are thought to boost eyesight health and help prevent heart disease.

“The greatest wealth is health.”
Virgil

Apple Cherry Blast

Ingredients

2 handfuls of shredded lettuce (romaine is best)

1 apple

1 banana

100g cherries

200ml coconut water (or plain water)

Ice cubes

Making It

Wash the ingredients. Chop up and core the apple. Remove the stones and stalks from the cherries. Put all the ingredients in the Nutribullet and add the water being careful not to go over the MAX line. Blend for 20 to 30 seconds or until smooth. If required add some more coconut or plain water.

Health Benefits

Cherries contain the highest levels of antioxidants of any fruit. Cherries are rich in flavonoids including anthocyanins which may help with boosting your memory. If you have trouble sleeping, cherries may be able to help, they are a good source of melatonin which can aid with a restful night's sleep. Cherries are also high in potassium which helps regulate blood pressure levels and your heart rate.

Romaine Lettuce contains all 9 essential amino acids. It is high in calcium, omega-3 essential fats and contains more vitamin A than a carrot. The water content of romaine lettuce helps to keep you hydrated and your skin clear. Try and pick a crispy fresh lettuce to use.

Fruit is fast food.

Honey & Lemon Smoothie

Ingredients

1 apple

1/2 pineapple

1 tsp of fresh grated root ginger

1/2 lemon (unwaxed)

1 tbsp of honey (Manuka if possible)

Water

Ice cubes

Making It

Wash, chop and remove seeds from the apple, remove the the skin from the pineapple. Add all the ingredients to the Nutribullet blender. If you are using an unwaxed organic lemon you can also blend the peel.

Fill up with water (without going over the MAX line) and blend for 20 to 30 seconds or until smooth. Add more water if required.

Health Benefits

Lemons are great at detoxing your body, the juice is a brilliant alkalizer for the body. Sometimes we can have too much acid in our bodies forcing our energy levels to drop and in turn our immune system. Lemons are rich in vitamin C which is not only good for staying healthy on the inside, but also for keeping skin clear and blemish free.

Ginger adds a delicious zing to any smoothie. The health benefits of ginger have been known by various different cultures for many centuries. The most well-known one is probably to treat nausea, especially in motion sickness and morning sickness. However, it is also thought that ginger, especially when eaten in raw form, might help with inflammation and sore muscles.

Fit is not a destination, it's a way of life.

Awesome Almond Smoothie

Ingredients

1 fresh mango (or 2 handfuls of frozen)

1 medium ripe banana

150ml of almond milk

1 handful of fresh almonds

Ice cubes (unless you are using frozen mango)

Making It

Peel and chop the mango (if using fresh), peel and chop the banana. Add all the ingredients to the Nutribullet blender cup.

Blend for about 20 to 30 seconds or until smooth. Add more water or almond milk if you require a thinner consistency.

Health Benefits

Mango is a popular fruit to add to a smoothie. I like to use freshly frozen mango chunks as they not only act as great ice cubes but they enable me to make a smoothie much more quickly. Mango is rich in flavonoids (especially beta-carotene) and vitamin A which is beneficial for maintaining a health eye-sight.

Mango is high in fibre and vitamin C, which is great for lowering cholesterol levels and boosting the immune system.

The high antioxidant properties of a mango make them a fantastic fruit to eat regularly. Isn't it great when something tastes so amazing *and* is good for you?

Almond milk is 100% plant based and rich in antioxidants. It is a great source of vitamin E which contributes to the protection of cells from oxidative stress. Not only that, almond milk is naturally low in fat and easy to digest due to it being naturally lactose free.

The smooth, creamy and nutty taste will add to the taste of any smoothie.

As long as you use an almond milk that is unsweetened with no additives, it will be low in carbohydrates, meaning that by using it you won't significantly increase your blood sugar levels. Other benefits include being low in sodium with no cholesterol or saturated fat. It is high in the healthy fats, including omega fatty acids. Almond milk is high in fibre, aiding the digestion of your smoothie. Vitamins include iron and riboflavin which are necessary for muscle growth and healing. Although almond milk only contains 1 gram of protein per serving, it contains plenty of B vitamins such as iron and riboflavin, both important for muscle growth and healing.

Almonds when consumed raw in a natural and unsalted form, they pack quite a nutritional punch. They are great to pop into a smoothie, or eaten as a snack during the day. Owing to their magnesium content, almonds are great for your heart health. Almonds are high in protein and fibre yet naturally low in sugar.

"It is health that is real wealth and not pieces of gold and silver."
Mahatma Gandhi

Berry Coconut Smoothie

Ingredients

1 tbsp coconut oil (try for best quality virgin raw – see below for details)

2 handfuls of mixed fresh or frozen berries of your choice

250ml of coconut water

Ice cubes (unless using frozen berries)

Making It

Add the berries (wash if using fresh), coconut water and ice cubes (but not the coconut oil). Blend for 20 to 30 seconds or until smooth.

One of the problems of adding coconut oil to a smoothie is that it can clump into a ball when it reaches your cold smoothie. That is because coconut oil solidifies when it is cold, which does not make for a delicious tasting smoothie! The ice cubes and frozen fruits used in this recipe will add to the problem, but in my opinion, a cold smoothie is much nicer than a room temperature one! To avoid this potential problem you can gently heat the coconut oil to melt it to liquid form before adding it.

I would recommend blending all the ingredients and then once smooth add the melted coconut oil to the Nutribullet and blend again. Add more water or coconut water until you are happy with the consistency.

Health Benefits

You have probably seen the hype surrounding **coconut oil** lately. It is a great ingredient to add to your smoothie as it provides multiple health benefits. Although virgin coconut oil is a saturated fat, it can actually help promote good health. Virgin coconut oil contains medium chain fatty acids. They are easier to digest than other saturated fats and are metabolised faster. They are used as a source of energy rather than being converted to and stored as fat. Make sure the product you purchase is unrefined or you will lose many of the benefits of it.

Coconut oil contains no cholesterol and has fewer calories by weight than any other fat source. It is also rich in vitamin C, zinc, magnesium, potassium and folate.

Virgin coconut oil is also said to be soothing for sunburn and skin conditions when applied directly to the skin. You can also use it to fry and roast your foods instead of using another type of cooking oil.

"**The drugstore in a bottle**" is how *coconut oil* is now called in the Philippines where virgin oil has been creating literally an "explosion" of the sick and not so sick treating every imaginable disease with this oil - and achieving, unbelievably rapid relief and cures"

Conrado S. Dayrit, MD, FACC, FPCC, FPCP,
Emeritus Professor of Pharmacology,
University of the Philippines, College of Medicine

SKIN BOOSTING SMOOTHIES

Drinking a smoothie is a fantastic way to give your skin a really fab boost. Your skin really does tell a tale about how things are going on inside you. If you are consuming a diet high in processed foods and sugars, lacking in fruit, vegetables, nuts and seeds, your skin will probably be looking puffy, wrinkly and with blemishes/spots.

Your skin really needs antioxidants, essential fatty acids and other nutrients on a daily basis to keep you looking young, healthy and full of life!

Always keep some water on hand during the day, we really do need to keep hydrated and your skin will reward you for it.

Alongside water, coconut water is another brilliant fluid to consume – the high levels of potassium help to cleanse the toxins within, the results will speak for themselves with vibrant and younger looking skin.

Top Tips for Healthier Skin

Aside from incorporating the following smoothies into your daily diet, try to consider some of the following tips;

- Avoid or limit your consumption of caffeine, processed sugar, salt, alcohol and nicotine
- Use sun cream appropriate for your skin type
- Drink lots of water every day (at least 1 litre)
- Get a good night's sleep
- Snack on fresh fruit, vegetables, nuts and seeds.

Clearly Cashew

Ingredients

1 apple

1 handful of unsalted cashew nuts

1 banana

1 tsp spirulina (optional)

250ml of coconut water

Ice cubes

Making It

Wash, chop and core the apple. Add all the ingredients to the Nutribullet blender taking care not to go over the MAX line. Blend for about 20 to 30 seconds or until smooth. Add more coconut water or plain water if you require a thinner consistency.

Health Benefits

Cashew nuts are not only a great energy boost, they are also beneficial to your skin. They are high in protein, healthy fats and many vitamins. Cashew nuts are high in zinc and selenium which is said to be helpful in reducing acne.

Spirulina can be bought in most health food stores or online. Spirulina is known as a superfood owing to the staggering amount of nutrients found within it. It has large concentrated amounts of beta-carotene, iron and vitamin B-12. Spirulina is also rich in GLA (gamma-linolenic acid), an essential fatty acid which is great for health and vibrant looking skin.

"If you keep good food in your fridge, you will eat good food"

Errick McAdams

Cleansing Cucumber

Ingredients

1 handful of romaine lettuce

1 apple

1/2 cucumber

Half a lime

Water

Ice cubes

Making It

Wash, chop and core the apple, wash the cucumber and romaine lettuce. Cut the lime in half. Add all the ingredients to the Nutribullet blender and top up with water, taking care not to go over the MAX line. Blend for about 20 to 30 seconds or until smooth. Add more water if you require a thinner consistency.

Health Benefits

Cucumbers have a whopping 90% water content. Only a watermelon contains more. On a hot day, cucumbers (and watermelons) are fantastic thirst quenchers. Keeping well hydrated is a sure way to get healthy looking skin. They are also great to consume before and after a workout. Try and use organic cucumbers if you can so that you can blend the skin too. High levels of silica are found in the skin, a mineral that can strengthen muscles, ligaments, skin, bones, cartilage and tendons.

Cucumbers are also high in vitamin K, an antioxidant useful for those prone to dark circles under their eyes. Just place a slice on each eye and leave them there for about 20 minutes.

Romaine lettuce contains all 9 essential amino acids making is a great nutritional base for your smoothie. Not only that, it is also high in omega-3 essential fats, calcium and vitamin A. Just a handful of romaine lettuce will provide you with all your daily requirements of vitamin A which helps to revitalise the skin. The potassium found in the lettuce assists with circulation, boosting skin health. Like the cucumber, the high water content is perfect for keeping your skin hydrated and healthy looking.

Sumptuous Strawberries

Ingredients

1 handful of spinach

2 handfuls of fresh or frozen strawberries

1 tbsp of ground flaxseeds

Water

Ice cubes

Making It

Wash the spinach and strawberries (unless using frozen) and add all the ingredients to the Nutribullet blender, topping up with water, taking care not to go over the MAX line. Blend for about 20 to 30 seconds or until smooth. Add more water if you require a thinner consistency.

Health Benefits

Strawberries contain high levels of vitamin C, more so per serving than an orange. Vitamin C helps combat wrinkles and dry skin. Strawberries are also high in the antioxidant ellagic acid which is thought to help keep the skin elastic and firm.

Ground flaxseeds are rich in omega 3 fatty acids which are brilliant for keeping your skin hydrated, soft and smooth looking as well as treating acne and other skin allergies.

Popeye gulped it back to make his muscles bulge, but he may not have known that **spinach** is a fantastic green leaf vegetable to consume for healthy and vibrant looking skin. It is low in calories and high in magnesium, a mineral that promotes healthy skin and bones. It is also high in vitamins A, C and K.

“Your body is a temple. But only if you treat it like one.”

Astrid Alauda

Beautiful Blueberry

Ingredients

1 handful of fresh or frozen blueberries

1 apple

1 pear

1 tbsp of ground flaxseeds

250ml of coconut water

Ice cubes

Making It

Wash the blueberries (if using fresh), pear and apple. Chop and core the apple and pear and place all the ingredients in the ingredients to the Nutribullet blender taking care not to go over the MAX line. Blend for about 20 to 30 seconds or until smooth. Add more water or coconut water if you require a thinner consistency.

Health Benefits

Apples are great for cleaning the colon and getting your skin looking clear. They are full of vitamin C which is fantastic for your skin complexion. Apples also contain vitamin B which is good for skin problems.

Pears are an anti-aging fruit that can really boost your skin's appearance and health. Pears contain a lot of fibre, helping to keep your complexion looking smooth.

Blueberries are high in numerous vitamins and minerals helping to slow down the signs of ageing. The nutrients found in blueberries will help with those suffering from acne and blotchy skin conditions. The vitamin C found in blueberries helps to strengthen the blood vessels found just below the surface of your skin, reducing the risk of broken capillaries appearing.

Fuel your body. Fuel your life.

Strawberry & Cashew

Ingredients

1 handful of romaine lettuce

1/4 pineapple (fresh or frozen)

1 handful of fresh or frozen strawberries

1 handful of cashew nuts

Water

Ice cubes

Making It

Wash the lettuce and strawberries (if using fresh). Peel the pineapple and chop up. Place all the ingredients in the ingredients to the Nutribullet blender and top up with water, taking care not to go over the MAX line. Blend for about 20 to 30 seconds or until smooth. Add more water if you require a thinner consistency.

Health Benefits

Pineapple contains vitamin C and amino acids, nutrients which are beneficial for healthy looking skin. Pineapple increases collagen which will help with the skin's elasticity. As you age, your body will produce less collagen, which will make your skin more prone to sagging and appear less firm. Pineapple is rich in vitamin C which is useful for fighting acne outbreaks.

Cashew Nuts are rich in selenium and zinc. Selenium works alongside vitamin E which helps to hydrate the skin and reduce skin inflammation. Zinc is great for the immune system and cell growth, helping to renew skin that may have been damaged previously.

Eat like you love yourself.

Strawberry Shine

Ingredients

1/2 avocado

1 banana

1 handful of strawberries (fresh or frozen)

250ml water/nut milk (almond milk is a good choice)

Ice cubes

Making It

The banana and avocado will make this smoothie even smoother. It may mean you need to add extra water or nut milk than usual as both these ingredients can cause a thicker consistency.

Peel the banana and avocado, scooping out the flesh of the avocado. Wash the strawberries (if using fresh ones) and add all the ingredients to the Nutribullet cup. Add the water or nut milk, being careful not to go over the MAX line. Blend for about 20 to 30 seconds or until smooth. Add more liquid (water or nut milk) if you prefer it thinner.

Health Benefits

Almond milk contains high levels of vitamin E, an antioxidant containing essential properties for the health of your skin. Almond milk is also rich in riboflavin which can assist the tissues of the skin use oxygen.

Avocados are well known for their health benefits, and in particular the monounsaturated fats present in an avocado are ideal for improving your skin tone. The antioxidant carotenoids help to protect your skin from the visible signs of aging, such as wrinkles. The vitamin C aids with the making of collagen and elastin which helps with firmness and elasticity of the skin.

Strawberries contain high levels of vitamin C, more so per serving than an orange. Vitamin C helps combat wrinkles and dry skin. Strawberries are also high in the antioxidant ellagic acid which is thought to help keep the skin elastic and firm.

Eat Good. Feel Good.

Lemon & Mint

Ingredients

1 handful of romaine lettuce

1 apple

½ lemon (organic and unwaxed)

¼ cucumber

1tbsp chopped mint

250ml of coconut water

Making It

Wash the lettuce, apple, lemon and cucumber. Chop and core the apple. Add all the ingredients to the Nutribullet blender cup taking care not to go over the MAX line. Blend for about 20 to 30 seconds or until smooth. Add more coconut water if you require a thinner consistency.

Health Benefits

Adding **mint** to a smoothie will add a unique twist to the taste. Nutritionally, mint will help to maintain healthy skin owing to its cleansing and detoxification effects.

Coconut water will naturally hydrate your skin. The antioxidants found in coconut water will help to keep your skin looking young and healthy. The compounds cytokinins are present in coconut water which are thought to slow down the aging process.

Lemons are great at detoxifying, cleaning your body on the inside, resulting in healthier and clearer skin on the outside. The vitamin C found in lemons helps to support healthy and glowing skin.

A healthy outside starts from the inside.

Sunflower Seed Smoothie

Ingredients

1 ripe banana

2 handfuls of mixed berries (frozen or fresh)

2 tablespoons of raw and shelled sunflower seeds

250ml water (or coconut water if you prefer)

Ice cubes

Making It

Add all the ingredients to the Nutribullet and blend for 20 to 30 seconds. Add more water or coconut water if you require a thinner consistency. Be careful not to go over the MAX line on the Nutribullet cup.

Health Benefits

Sunflower seeds are rich in protein, iron, calcium, potassium and vitamin E. Just 1 ounce (2 tablespoons) of sunflower seeds is about 75% of the RDA for vitamin E. Vitamin E is a key antioxidant for your skin and also a healthy heart. Vitamin E can only be stored in your body for a limited amount of time so it is important to include it in your diet on a regular basis. The antioxidant effects of sunflower seeds can help keep your skin in good condition and looking young.

"We are all golden sunflowers inside."
Allen Ginsberg

Awesome Almond Smoothie

Ingredients

1 medium, ripe banana

10 raw almonds (unsalted)

250ml almond milk

1 tablespoon of ground flaxseed (optional)

Ice cubes

Making It

Add all the ingredients to the Nutribullet and blend for about 20 to 30 seconds or until smooth. Add more almond milk (or water) if you require a thinner consistency. Take care not to go over the MAX line on the Nutribullet cup.

Health Benefits

Almonds are not only a fantastic source of fibre and protein, they are also high in vitamin E and zinc. Both vitamin E and zinc assist with maintaining healthy skin, hair and nails by helping your body to produce keratin.

Love the skin you are in.

Perfectly Pomegranate Smoothie

Ingredients

250ml pomegranate juice

1 satsuma

1 medium ripe banana

Ice cubes

Making It

Peel the skin from both the satsuma and banana. Add all the ingredients to the Nutribullet cup. Blend for about 20 to 30 seconds or until smooth. If you require a thinner consistency add some water.

TIP: If you can, purchase the not from concentrate pomegranate juice

Health Benefits

Pomegranate juice is rich in fibre, potassium, vitamin C and disease fighting antioxidants. One glass of pomegranate juice provides almost half of the daily needs of vitamins A, C and E and folic acid. The antioxidants in pomegranates can help fight fine lines & wrinkles.

Eat less sugar, you're sweet enough already.

ENERGY BOOSTING & SPORTS SMOOTHIES

A nutrient rich smoothie can be the ideal pick me up when your energy levels start to dwindle. Sometimes no matter how much sleep we get, we can still feel a little sleepy in the afternoon.

If you take part in a regular exercise routine, or play some sports, your body will need you to be feeding it properly.

Smoothies are a quick and satisfying way of filling yourself with the required vitamins and nutrients your body and mind needs to run at full steam.

Peanut & Honey Blast

Ingredients

2 ripe bananas

2tbsp of peanut butter

250ml almond milk

1 tsp of Manuka honey

Ice cubes

Making It

Add all the ingredients to the Nutribullet cup and blend for 20 to 30 seconds or until smooth. If you require a thinner consistency please add more almond milk or water.

Health Benefits

Manuka honey is a brilliant natural energy booster. It is made up of fructose and glucose, a carbohydrate responsible for your body's primary energy source.

Peanut butter contains a good amount of healthy fats and protein. Not only does the protein make you feel fuller for longer, it helps with repairing and building muscles.

"I really regret eating healthy today."

Said No One Ever

Beet It

Ingredients

1 handful of spinach (or romaine lettuce)

1 carrot

½ raw beetroot

Half a lemon (unwaxed)

250ml of water

Ice cubes

Making It

Depending on your taste buds, you might want to use beetroot juice rather than raw beetroot. I don't really like the taste of raw beetroot blended and so I pop it in my juicer and use the juice from it. Of course that means more washing up, or you might not have a juicer. With that in mind, you can buy beetroot juice from supermarkets and health shops, just make sure you go for brands that don't use concentrated and any added ingredients. If you are going to use beetroot juice, use about 250ml and don't add any water (unless you want a thinner consistency).

Wash the other ingredients and add to the Nutribullet. Blend for about 20 to 30 seconds or until smooth.

Health Benefits

The nitrate in **beetroot** converts into nitric oxide in our bodies providing us with longer lasting energy. Beetroot also enlarges the blood vessels, enabling oxygen to flow more easily, increasing stamina and energy. Beetroot juice is also a great natural remedy for anaemia due to the high iron content.

Your stomach shouldn't be a waste basket.

Totally Bananas

Ingredients

2 medium ripe bananas (these can be frozen)

1 apple

250ml almond milk (or coconut water/soya milk if you prefer)

1 pinch cinnamon

Ice cubes (unless using frozen bananas)

Making It

Chop and core the apple. Add all the ingredients to the Nutribullet blender cup and blend for 20 to 30 seconds or until smooth.

Health Benefits

Bananas are rich in complex carbohydrates, providing your body with instant and sustainable energy. This makes them an instant win when you are in need of more energy, especially before a workout.

Not only does **cinnamon** add a delicious twist to this smoothie, the spice can also help to reduce blood sugar levels.

Don't look back. You're not going that way.

Berry Nutty Smoothie

Ingredients

1 handful of spinach

2 handfuls of fresh or frozen mixed berries

5 Brazil nuts

250ml of coconut water (or plain water)

Ice cubes (unless using frozen berries)

Making It

Wash the ingredients and add to the Nutribullet cup. Blend for about 20 to 30 seconds, or until completely smooth. Add more liquid if you require a thinner consistency.

Health Benefits

Brazil nuts are perfect for both snacking and putting in a smoothie. They are high in healthy monounsaturated fats, protein, vitamin E, magnesium and selenium. The high levels of selenium found in Brazil nuts make them useful for maintaining a healthy immune system. Brazil nuts can help build and maintain strong bones and muscles, as well as aid the natural recovery process.

Let exercise be your stress reliever, not food.

Kicking Kiwi

Ingredients

2 handfuls of kale

1 kiwi

1 tbsp of honey

250ml soya milk (or a milk of your choice)

Ice cubes

Making It

Peel the kiwi. Add all the ingredients to the Nutribullet recipe book and blend for around 20 to 30 seconds or until smooth. If you require a thinner consistency add more liquid (milk or water).

Health Benefits

Kiwis are packed with vitamin C, making them a super power when it comes to boosting your immune system. Kiwis are also high in vitamin K, E and potassium.

You don't know your limits until you push yourself past them.

Wonderful Walnut Smoothie

Ingredients

1 banana
2 tbsps of chopped walnuts
1 handful of fresh or frozen raspberries

250ml of coconut water

Ice cubes

Making It

Add all the ingredients to the Nutribullet. Blend for 20 to 30 seconds or until smooth. Add more coconut water (or plain water) if you require a thinner consistency.

Health Benefits

Walnuts are a great source of magnesium and potassium, essential electrolytes for muscle function. They also contain the essential fatty acid linolenic. They are high in protein and fibre.

YOU control what your body looks like.

The Energy Boost

Ingredients

1/2 ripe avocado

Half pineapple (or 2 handfuls of chopped frozen)

1 handful of kale

250ml of coconut water (or plain water)

Ice cubes (unless using frozen pineapple)

Making It

Add all the ingredients to the Nutribullet and blend for about 20 to 30 seconds until smooth. Add more liquid if you require a thinner consistency.

Health Benefits

Coconut water is great to have after a workout to replace electrolytes lost through sweating.

Avocados are a fantastic source of energy when you have a workout planned. They are rich in monounsaturated fats which helps with muscle repair after taking part in sporting activity.

"I eat an avocado every day. It's amazing for your skin. It's one of the super-foods, and I'm just so into eating properly and healthily."

Joan Collins

Berry Boost

Ingredients

1 handful of fresh or frozen raspberries

1 handful of fresh or frozen blueberries

200ml oat milk

3 tablespoons of live natural yoghurt

1 tablespoon of honey

Making It

Add all the ingredients to the Nutribullet and blend for 20 to 30 seconds or until smooth. The consistency may be a bit thick – add more oat milk or water if required.

TIP: The darker the blueberry, the sweeter the taste.

Health Benefits

Oat milk has more vitamin A than cow's milk. It is also very high in iron which is great for energy levels, especially if you are prone to anaemia.

Blueberries are not only a great brain booster, they are also useful for keeping your physical energy levels high. Blueberries are also high in antioxidants making them a beneficial smoothie ingredient, as well as a useful fruit to snack on during the day.

"Have blueberries whenever you are low – destiny will change and you will be high"

Adam Voichester

Chia & Mango Smoothie

Ingredients

1 mango (or 2 handfuls of chopped frozen mango)

½ lime

250ml coconut water

1 teaspoon of chia seeds

Ice cubes

Making It

Add all the ingredients to the Nutribullet. A lot of the vitamins and nutrients are found in the skin of a lime so try to include the skin. If the taste feels too overwhelming, add just a couple of slices at a time. Blend for about 20 to 30 seconds or until smooth. Add more coconut water or plain water if required.

Health Benefits

Chia seeds are super healthy as they are rich in healthy omega-3 fatty acids, antioxidants, protein, calcium, fibre and various micro nutrients. Chia seeds are 40% fibre by weight, meaning they are one of the richest sources of fibre in the world.

Mangos add a deliciously creamy texture to your smoothie. They are high in potassium which is ideal for people working out (you lose potassium as you sweat.) Potassium helps to produce energy, athletic performance, muscle tissue regulation, muscle contraction and reduce fatigue.

Don't give up. One day you'll look back and be glad you didn't.

BREAKFAST SMOOTHIES

Having a smoothie with breakfast is the perfect way to start the day. I love the thought that I have consumed so many vitamins and nutrients before I've even started the day. I like to have a healthy smoothie alongside a yummy egg or muesli breakfast.

Depending on what is in it, you can even have the smoothie as your breakfast. Just try and choose something that will keep you feeling fuller and release energy slowly throughout the morning.

If you are trying to lose weight, having a smoothie for breakfast (and lunch) is a good meal replacement. I like to double up and make enough to have for breakfast and lunch, that way I only have to prepare it once!

Benefits of having something for breakfast include;

- Increased metabolism
- Enhanced mood
- Help maintain or lose weight
- Improved concentration and focus
- Enhanced immune system

Muesli & Banana Smoothie

Ingredients

1 pear

1 banana

50g muesli

1 tbsp natural maple syrup

200ml unsweetened soya milk

Making It

Wash the pear and remove the core. Keep the skin on and add to the Nutribullet. Add the remaining ingredients and blend for 20 to 30 seconds or until smooth. Add more water or soya milk if you require a thinner consistency.

TIP: Making your own muesli is cheaper than buying from the supermarket. Plus, you can customise it to your taste.

Health Benefits

Maple syrup is very high in (natural) sugar so should only be consumed in small amounts. As far as sweeteners go though, it is better for you than refined sugar. Maple syrup does however contain many different kinds of antioxidants, and the darker the syrup, the more beneficial.

Muesli is high in fibre and whole grains which is useful for making you feel fuller for longer. Make sure you buy (or you can make your own) muesli that only has whole oats, dried fruits, nuts and wheat flakes. The nuts in muesli make it a great source of protein. If you are making your own it is preferable to leave out the dried fruit as it is high in sugar.

Wake up each day with the belief that some amazing is going to happen.

Breakfast Boost

Ingredients

2 tbsp oats

1 tbsp plain live yoghurt

2 handfuls of mixed berries (fresh or frozen)

250ml unsweetened almond milk

Ice cubes (unless using frozen berries)

Making It

Add all the ingredients to the Nutribullet and blend for 20 to 30 seconds. Add more almond milk (or water) for a thinner consistency.

Health Benefits

Oats are a fantastic filling for any smoothie. They are a great source of protein, high in calcium, magnesium and potassium. Oats are also high in soluble fibre which will leave you feeling fuller for longer, as well as help lower bad cholesterol.

Natural yoghurt has the highest level of calcium and is the simplest form of yoghurt. Yoghurt is also high in protein and potassium. Yoghurt is a good source of various vitamins and minerals.

Eat well for breakfast and you will shine all day long.

Strawberry & Banana Smoothie

Ingredients

12 strawberries (fresh or frozen)

1 banana

4 tbsp wheat germ

250ml of unsweetened almond milk or coconut water

Ice cubes

Making It

Wash the strawberries and cut off the green tops. Add all the ingredients to the Nutribullet blender. Blend for about 20 to 30 seconds or until smooth. Add more liquid if you require a thinner consistency.

TIP: If you buy wheat germ in bulk it can be split up into food bags and stored in the freezer for up to 2 months.

Health Benefits

Wheat germ can be bought in all good health shops, supermarkets and online. Wheat germ is high in essential fatty acids, vitamin B, amino acids, fibre, iron and vitamin E. Wheat germ is incredibly nutrient rich and is a fantastic source of energy to get your day off to a positive start.

Bananas (and wheat germ) contain vitamin B6 which helps to convert food into energy. It also assists your body in producing serotonin which can aid with alleviating anxiety and depression.

"Most people have no idea how good their body is designed to feel."

Kevin Trudeau

Berry Breakfast

Ingredients

1 handful of strawberries

1 handful of raspberries

1 handful of blueberries

250ml of coconut water

Ice cubes (unless using frozen berries)

Making It

I like to keep a selection of mixed berries in the freezer so that I can make this smoothie all year round, when I want to. Most supermarkets sell packets of frozen fruits now so they should be easy to get hold of.

Put all the ingredients in the Nutribullet and blend for about 20 to 30 seconds or until smooth. Add more liquid if you require a thinner consistency.

Health Benefits

Berries are high in antioxidants which can help to reduce inflammation, slow down age-related memory loss, improve joint flexibility, skin and hair health. Berries are also low in calories, high in fibre and taste delicious.

"Start the day by doing what's necessary; then do what's possible; and suddenly you're doing the impossible."

Francis of Assisi

Peanut B Breakfast Smoothie

Ingredients

1 banana (chopped and frozen works great)

1 tbsp peanut butter

200ml soya milk (or your choice of milk)

Ice cubes

Making It

Add the ingredients to the Nutribullet and blend for about 20 to 30 seconds. If you require a thinner consistency add more milk.

Health Benefits

Peanut butter is a great breakfast inclusion owing to its high protein and fibre content, making you feel fuller for longer. It is also rich in vitamin E, a powerful antioxidant which helps to maintain a healthy blood supply. The magnesium in peanut butter is an all-round energy booster and helps to keeps bones strong. Check the label before buying though, you want low sodium and try to go for a natural peanut butter brand with less sugar content.

"Either you run the day or the day runs you."

Jim Rohn

Strawberry Burst

Ingredients

1 small ripe banana

100g strawberries (about 8-10 large ones)

150ml of freshly squeezed orange juice

Ice cubes

Making It

Add all the ingredients to the blender. I like to use frozen strawberries and then there is no need for ice cubes. It also means I can eat strawberries out of season.

Blend for 20 to 30 seconds or until smooth. Add more liquid (orange juice or water) if you require a thinner consistency.

Health Benefits

This is a great smoothie to have for breakfast, the high carbohydrate yet low fat ingredients will keep you feeling full of energy. The potassium found in **bananas** is a vital mineral for muscle and nerve function. The high fibre of the **strawberries** (found in the flesh and the seeds) will help keep your digestive tract healthy.

Strawberries are the only fruits to wear their seeds on the outside. There are 200 seeds on the average strawberry!

Kindly Kiwi

Ingredients

3 ripe kiwis

1 small ripe banana

250ml coconut water

Ice cubes

Making It

Peel the kiwis and banana and add all the ingredients to the blender. Blend for 20 to 30 seconds or until smooth. If you require a thinner consistency add more coconut water (or plain water).

Health Benefits

Kiwis are a great breakfast option. They are very high in vitamin C (even higher than oranges), vitamin E, potassium and the soluble fibre, pectin. The seeds are also a brilliant source of omega 3 fatty acids.

I am ready to enjoy perfect health.

Awakening Avocado

Ingredients

1 small avocado (or ½ large one)

1 handful of spinach

1 small ripe banana

1 tsp of honey (optional)

250ml almond milk (or milk of your choice)

Ice cubes

Making It

Cut the avocado in half and scoop out the flesh. Add it to the blender with all the other ingredients. Blend for 20 to 30 seconds, or until smooth. If you require a thinner consistency add more milk.

When choosing an avocado, make sure it is ripe enough by giving it a little squeeze, it should give slightly if it is ready. I'm not so keen on little bits of avocado floating around in my smoothie!

Health Benefits

Avocados are a beneficial fruit (yes, technically they are classed as a fruit!) to have at any time of the day. Nut there is something satisfying knowing that you have consumed such a powerhouse of nutritional benefits at the beginning of the day. Avocados are high in monounsaturated "good" fats. They are also abundantly rich in protein, vitamins, minerals, antioxidants and fibre.

"The avocado is a food without rival among the fruits, the veritable fruit of paradise."

David Fairchild

Mango Morning

Ingredients

1 ripe mango (or 100g of frozen chopped)

1 tsp fresh grated ginger

250ml coconut water

Ice cubes

Making It

Scoop out the flesh of the mango. I find it easier to use chopped frozen mango straight from the freezer. Most supermarkets sell them in their frozen desserts section. Add all the other ingredients and blend for about 20 to 30 seconds or until smooth. If you require a thinner consistency add more coconut water or normal water.

Health Benefits

Ginger has a wide variety of health benefits and add a warming zing to any smoothie. Most people know ginger as a remedy for nausea and stomach aches. It can also help with congestion and relieve general symptoms of the cold and flu. The anti-inflammatory properties of ginger may assist with reducing muscle soreness.

Developing healthy eating habits gets easier each day.

Cinnamon Breakfast Smoothie

Ingredients

1 medium ripe banana

100g (or about 12 large) strawberries

½ tsp ground cinnamon

1 tbsp maple syrup or raw honey

200ml soya milk (or milk of your choice)

Ice cubes

Making It

If you have frozen bananas and strawberries this works really well, just throw it all in the blender with no need for ice cubes and whizz for 20 to 30 seconds. Add more liquid (milk or water) if you want a thinner consistency.

Health Benefits

Not only is **cinnamon** a delicious spice to add to a smoothie, it is thought that it may help lower blood sugar levels. It can also have an anti-inflammatory effect on the body, helping to relieve pain.

Your attitude determines your direction.

TREAT SWEET SMOOTHIES

Are you one of those people who *needs* something sweet every once in a while? Let's be honest – anything likely to satisfy that sweet tooth craving is unlikely to pass as a healthy option, however by harnessing natures natural sweetness it CAN be achieved!

More often than not, your 'sweet tooth' will strike at the most inopportune moment and before you know it you have reached for the chocolate bar, trifle or cream cake. The key here is to be prepared when you do your weekly shop and ensure you have adequate supplies, so you are not tempted by the high sugar, high calorific option instead.

Healthy sweeter option smoothies that we have made in the course of writing this book, have more than satisfied my ferocious sweet tooth but left me feeling less bloated and sluggish, than that of traditional highly processed sugary dessert.

The following taste bud tingling recipes will give you the chance to satisfy your sugar craving with impunity.

Cheeky Chocolate Smoothie

Ingredients

2 chunks of grated dark chocolate (minimum 75% cocoa content)

1 medium ripe banana (can use frozen)

200ml unsweetened almond milk (or any other nut milk / soya milk)

1 handful of kale

Ice cubes (unless using frozen banana)

Making It

Rinse the kale and place all the ingredients in the Nutribullet and blend for about 20 to 30 seconds. If you prefer a thinner consistency add some more milk or water.

Health Benefits

Contrary to popular belief **dark chocolate**, with a cocoa content of 70% has been medically proven to offer us a host of health benefits including heart, circulation and brain function. Dark chocolate can help restore flexibility to the arteries.

As well as curbing that sweet chocolate craving, good quality, high cocoa chocolate can be very nutritious and is packed with beneficial minerals such as potassium, zinc and selenium, and a 100g bar of dark (70 per cent or more) choc provides 67 per cent of the RDA of iron. So go on, and enjoy it!

Run like chocolate is at the finish line.

Raspberry & Banana Smoothie

Ingredients

1 handful of fresh or frozen raspberries

1 medium ripe banana

1 handful of spinach

200ml water

Ice Cubes

Making It

If you are using fresh raspberries, then rinse first and place in the cup. I tend to keep a tub of frozen raspberries in the freezer so that I can use them all year round. Add the other ingredients, half the water and blend well. Add more water gradually until you have the consistency required.

Health Benefits

Raspberries have a lot going for them. Not only do they taste delicious and deliver that sweet kick, but they are also packed to the brim with vitamins, nutrients and minerals. They are also low in fat and calories, but rich in dietary fibre and antioxidants such as vitamin C, Quercetin and gallic acid. These antioxidants can help to fight against cancer, heart and circulatory disease and age-related decline. Raspberries have been shown to have anti-inflammatory properties.

Don't let anyone ever dull your sparkle.

Tropical Treat

Ingredients

¼ chopped pineapple

1 handful of fresh or frozen mango

2 medium carrots

200ml water

Ice cubes

Making It

Peel the pineapple, carrots and mango (if using fresh mango) then place all ingredients in the Nutribullet cup and blend. Add more water if you require a thinner consistency.

Health Benefits

Mango is rich in vitamin A and flavonoids, including beta-carotene which is great for good eye health and vision, plus it can help boost your immune system. The sweet taste means it is a firm favourite in our house with both the adults and the children. The high dietary fibre content of mangoes make them a great ingredient to also use in weight loss smoothies.

Pineapples are the only source of the plant compound, bromelain. Bromelain is associated with many health benefits, such as enhanced immune function, cancer prevention, improved wound healing and better gut health.

"It is health that is real wealth and not pieces of gold and silver."

Mahatma Gandhi

Perfectly Peach Smoothie

Ingredients

2 peaches

1 handful of fresh or frozen mango

200ml of water

Ice cubes

Making It

Peel peaches and remove stones. Place all the ingredients in your Nutribullet and blend for about 20 to 30 seconds. For variety you can always substitute water for coconut water or unsweetened nut milk.

Health Benefits

Peaches are native to China and are packed with low calorie goodness but delivering a super sweet kick. They are rich in vitamin A, beta-carotene and vitamin c (ascorbic acid).

Vitamins A and C not only help to aid healthy eyes and vision but are also great for your skin too.

Dried peaches are a great source of iron.

It's a good day to have a good day.

Mighty Mango Smoothie

Ingredients

1 banana

1 apple

1 handful of fresh or frozen mango

250ml of coconut water or plain water

Ice cubes (unless using frozen mango)

Making It

Wash and core the apple. If using fresh mango, peel the skin and scoop out the flesh. Chop the banana and add all the ingredients to the Nutribullet cup and blend together for 20 to 30 seconds or until smooth. Add more liquid if you prefer a thinner consistency.

Health Benefits

Mangoes are rich in beta-carotene which can help with acne and lack lustre looking skin.

Foods rich in beta-carotene are usually found in orange, yellow and red hued fruits and vegetables including: sweet potatoes, carrots and peppers.

Today is the perfect day to start living your dreams.

Super Blueberries

Ingredients

2 handfuls of fresh or frozen blueberries

½ medium ripe banana

250ml unsweetened almond milk

Ice cubes

Making It

If you are using fresh blueberries, then rinse them well, before adding all the ingredients to the Nutribullet cup and blend well. If you do not like almond milk, then feel free to substitute it for coconut milk or plain water. If you require a thinner consistency add more milk or water.

Health Benefits

Blueberries are a popular superfood and packed with vitamins, minerals and have more antioxidants per serving than all other fruits, vegetables, spices and seasonings.

Antioxidants are compounds in foods that neutralize chemicals called free radicals (unstable molecules) and are said to help protect against many health issues, including heart disease, stroke and gum disease amongst others.

Blueberries can help slow down the signs of aging and help improve your memory, now that's a SUPER food!

"Few die of hunger. Many die of eating."
Benjamin Franklin

Chocolate & Raspberry Pudding Smoothie

Ingredients

2 chunks of grated dark chocolate (minimum of 75% cocoa content)

1 handful of frozen raspberries

1 tablespoon of peanut butter (natural if possible)

250ml of coconut water

Ice cubes

Making It

Grate the chocolate chunks and place all the ingredients in the Nutribullet cup. Blend for about 20 to 30 seconds, adding more liquid if you prefer a thinner consistency. Coconut water can be substituted with water if preferred.

Health Benefits

Natural **peanut butter** has around 75% unsaturated fats which helps keep your heart healthy.

Most of us have way too much sodium in our diets and as you probably already know, sodium can wreak havoc on your cardiovascular system.

Peanut butter acts as an excellent source of potassium, and potassium can go a long way towards countering the dangers of sodium. Natural peanut butter is a great addition to any smoothie.

The protein and unsaturated fat content can help to keep you feeling fuller for longer.

"Health is a relationship between you and your body."

Terri Guillemets

Zingy Ginger Smoothie

Ingredients

¼ cucumber

2 carrots

1 tbsp freshly grated root ginger

½ unwaxed lemon

1 tbsp honey (raw or Manuka if possible)

200ml water

Ice cubes

Making It

If you are not using unwaxed lemons then you will need to peel the lemon and just add the flesh to the Nutribullet cup. Wash all the other ingredients, grate the ginger, chop the carrots and cucumber. Add all the ingredients with the water, taking care not to go over the MAX line. Blend for around 20 to 30 seconds. Add more water if required.

Health Benefits

Fresh root **ginger** has a very long history of use in various forms of traditional/alternative medicine. It has been used to help indigestion, unsettled stomachs, reduce nausea.

The soothing properties of ginger are also favourite natural remedy for colds.

Cucumbers contain an anti-inflammatory flavonol called fisetin that appears to play an important role in brain health.

"Every time you eat or drink, you are either feeding disease or fighting it."

Heather Morgan

Kiwi & Orange Smoothie

Ingredients

Juice from 2 oranges

1 pear

2 kiwi fruits

Water

Ice cubes

Making It

Juice two oranges, or if you do not mind the bits, simply peel and put the whole oranges in the Nutribullet cup. Peel and cut the kiwis. Chop the pear, but leave the skin on and add all the ingredients to the cup. Top up with water taking care not to go over the MAX line. Blend for around 20 to 30 seconds. Add more water if required.

Health Benefits

This zesty recipe harnesses the power of the humble **Kiwi**, which is a nutrient dense food, meaning they are high in nutrients and low in calories. It is also an excellent source of vitamin C, vitamin K as well as a very good source of copper and dietary fibre. It is also a good source of vitamin E, potassium, folate, and manganese.

Vitamin K has several important functions. For example, it's needed for blood clotting, which means it helps wounds to heal properly.

Pears contain certain flavonoids that can improve insulin sensitivity, which has been associated with a decrease in the risk of type 2 diabetes in both men and women.

"My motto in our household is that is 90% of your diet is healthy, that 10% just doesn't kill you."

Michelle Obama

Peachy Lemonade

Ingredients

2 peaches

1 apple

Juice of half a lemon

100ml of coconut water

150ml of carbonated water (sparkling water)

Ice cubes

Making It

Peel and remove the stone from the peach. Core the apple and cut it up. Place all the ingredients in to the Nutribullet cup, apart from the carbonated water. Blend for around 20 to 30 seconds, then add the carbonated water to turn this delicious drink into a lemonade style drink that everyone will love, especially the children.

Health Benefits

The health benefits of **lemons** have been known for centuries. The two biggest are lemons' strong antibacterial, antiviral, and immune-boosting powers and their use as a weight loss aid because lemon juice is a digestive aid and liver cleanser.

A simple squeeze of lemon can add a pleasant kick to even the sweetest of smoothies.

Coconut water is a natural isotonic drink that provides many of the same benefits as formulated sports drinks, including the electrolytes calcium, magnesium, phosphorus, sodium and potassium, but in their natural form. Perfect for before and after sport.

You will never find what works for you until you STICK TO IT.

GREEN SMOOTHIES

Green smoothies are a delicious blended drink made from fruit and leafy greens that can be very tasty. We have all heard at some point if we want to be healthy, one thing we should definitely do is eat more greens.

Lots of us simply don't like greens. I am the first to admit that when I first heard about green smoothies I thought, yuck! The news is I'm a convert. Not only do they taste great, but the benefits are amazing.

I am consuming so much more avocado, spinach and kale than I ever could in a usual meal. It is really satisfying to know that I am filling my body with so many rich and amazing nutrients all at the same time – and enjoying it too!

Top Tip- to make sure your green smoothies taste great always use ripe fruit.

Enjoy your greens!

Go Green Go

Ingredients

1 small ripe banana

1 handful of kale

1 handful of spinach

1 apple

1 tbsp of ground flaxseeds

Water

Ice cubes

Making It

Wash all the ingredients and place in the Nutribullet. Add the water taking care not to go over the MAX line. Blend until it reaches a smooth consistency. Add more water and ice as required.

Top Tip – Adding an apple to a green smoothie will help make it taste sweeter (I like to use Gala as they are sweeter).

Health Benefits

Of all the super healthy greens, **kale** is king. It is definitely one of the healthiest and most nutritious plant foods in existence. Kale is loaded with all sorts of beneficial compounds, some of which have powerful medicinal properties.

Kale can help lower cholesterol, which may reduce the risk of heart disease. Kale contains substances that bind bile acids and lower cholesterol levels in the body. Also kale is one of the world's best sources of vitamin K, with a single raw cup containing **almost 7 times** the recommended daily amount!

One small positive thought in the morning can change your whole day.

The Avocado Smoothie

Ingredients

1/2 medium ripe avocado

1/3 cucumber

1 handful of spinach

Juice of 1 lime

250ml of coconut water

Ice cubes

Making It

Scoop out the flesh of the avocado and then squeeze the juice from the lime. Wash the spinach and cucumber. Place all the ingredients into the NutriBullet and blend for about 20 to 30 seconds or until smooth. Add more water if necessary.

Health Benefits

This smoothie contains some powerful super foods loaded with tons of nutrients. Take **spinach** for example, it's important for your skin and hair, bone health, and it provides lots of protein, iron, vitamins and minerals.

Personally I love this smoothie. The combination of all the green goodness really makes me feel like my body is getting all the nutrients I need. Individually they are all ingredients I wouldn't really eat, but combined in a tasty smoothie it's a winner!

In life, much like smoothies, you get out what you put in.

Pineapple & Kale Crunch

Ingredients

1/2 medium ripe banana

2 handfuls of kale

1/2 medium pineapple

250ml coconut water

Ice cubes

Making It

Wash the kale, peel and cut the pineapple and banana. Place all the ingredients in to the NutriBullet and blend for 20 to 30 seconds. If required add more coconut water or plain water.

Health Benefits

The prime benefit of **kale** is its high nutrient content. Kale is a very good source of dietary fibre, calcium, manganese, copper, and potassium, as well as being particularly rich in vitamins A, C, and B6. One cup of kale contains over 200% of the daily recommended intake of vitamin A, an important nutrient for vision.

"There are two types of people; those who eat kale and those who should."

Bo Muller-Moore

Green Apple Smoothie

Ingredients

2 apples (Golden Delicious or Granny Smiths work well)

Large handful of spinach

½ lemon (unwaxed)

200ml coconut water or plain water

Ice cubes

Making It

Wash, core and chop the apples. Wash the spinach and lemon. Put all the ingredients in the Nutribullet blender. Blend for about 20 to 30 seconds or until smooth. Add more water if you require a thinner consistency.

Health Benefits

The **apple** is a wonderful fruit that is packed with rich phytol-nutrients that are indispensable for optimal health. Certain antioxidants in apples have several health promoting and disease prevention properties.

Lemon juice is a great alkalizer for the body. Did you know when we have too much acid in our body our energy levels drop and our immune systems do not work at their full ability? Lemon is said to be great at detoxing your body.

A great drink that I have grown to love is hot water with the juice of half a lemon. It is meant to improve liver function and help eliminate kidney stones.

You won't leave many footprints in the sand if you are just sitting.

Super Green Machine

Ingredients

1 apple

1 large carrot

1 handful of spinach

1 handful of kale

1 tbsp of mixed seeds

250ml of coconut water

Ice cubes

Making It

Wash, core and chop the apple. Wash the other ingredients and everything to the Nutribullet blender. Blend for about 20 to 30 seconds or until smooth. Top up with more water if needed.

Health Benefits

Kale and **spinach** are both so incredibly good for you, with so many health benefits. Kale can help lower cholesterol levels. Kale is low in calories, high in fibre and has zero fat. Spinach has high levels of potassium and low levels of sodium, the composition of these minerals helps to lower blood pressure.

Western culture's understanding of carrots being "good for the eyes" is one of the few we got right. Carrots are rich in beta-carotene, which is converted into vitamin A in the liver. Vitamin A is transformed in the retina, to rhodopsin, a purple pigment necessary for night vision.

"Every accomplishment starts with the decision to try."

Gail Devers

Abundantly Green Smoothie

Ingredients

1 apple

1 handful of spinach

1 handful of fresh or frozen blueberries

1 tbsp ground flaxseeds

1 tbsp of honey

Water

Ice cubes

Making It

Wash, core and chop the apple. Wash the other ingredients and add everything to the Nutribullet blender. Top up with water to the MAX line and blend for 20 to 30 seconds. Add more water if the smoothie is too thick. Blend again until smooth.

Top Tip: Only rinse blue berries right before you use them. Water increases the likelihood that they'll start to mold.

Health Benefits

You can add a tablespoon of **ground flaxseeds** to any smoothie (but don't have more than 2 tablespoons in a day as the husks contain compounds that can be toxic in high doses.) The amazing health giving properties of flaxseed are recognized around the world. They are a rich source of dietary fibre which can help relieve constipation. Other benefits include essential fatty acids, in particular omega 3 and omega 6.

It's no coincidence that four of the six letter of health are "heal."

Ed Northstrum

Apricot and Spinach Smoothie

Ingredients

3 ready to eat dried apricots

2 handfuls of spinach

1 large carrot

1/2 lemon (unwaxed)

250ml coconut water

Ice cubes

Making It

Wash the spinach, carrot and lemon. Add all the ingredients to the Nutribullet taking care not to go over the MAX line. Blend for about 20 to 30 seconds. If you prefer a thinner consistency add more water.

Health Benefits

Apricots are rich in carotenoids and xanthophylls, nutrients that researchers believe may help protect eyesight from age related damage.

Also, dried apricots are another great source of iron, meaning this smoothie will do wonders for your iron, and in turn, energy levels!

"Change the way you look at things and the things you look at change."

Wayne Dyer

✓ Yum!

Great Green Smoothie

Ingredients

1/4 cucumber

1/4 medium pineapple

1/2 ripe avocado

1 handful of kale

250ml coconut water

Ice cubes

Making It

Scoop out the flesh from a ripe avocado. Peel and cut the pineapple. Wash the cucumber and kale. Put all the ingredients in the Nutribullet taking care not to go over the MAX line. Blend for about 20 to 30 seconds. Add more liquid as desired.

Health Benefits

The **avocado** is an amazing fruit. It is an anti-ageing powerhouse, lowers bad cholesterol and is also fibre rich.

Also this fruit has clearly been shown to provide a wide variety of antioxidant and anti-inflammatory nutrients. Nutrients like manganese, vitamin C, and vitamin E, as well as phytonutrients like unique carotenoids, flavonoids, and phytosterols.

Nothing is impossible. The word itself says 'I'm Possible.'

Audrey Hepburn

Berry Avocado Smoothie

Ingredients

1/2 ripe avocado

¼ cucumber

1 cup/100g of mixed berries (raspberries and blackberries are good)

1 small ripe banana

Water

Ice cubes

Making It

Scoop out the flesh from half of the avocado. Add all the ingredients to the Nutribullet and top up with water without going over the MAX line. Blend until smooth. Add more water if you prefer a thinner consistency.

Health Benefits

Cucumbers are an excellent source of vitamin K and molybdenum. Also they are good for your nails. They contain the important nail health-promoting mineral silica

"The starting point of all achievement is desire."

Napolean Hill

Broccoli Smoothie

Ingredients

3-5 broccoli florets

1 handful spinach

1 medium carrot

1 apple

Water

Ice cubes

Making It

Wash the broccoli, spinach and carrot. Wash, chop and core the apple. Add all the ingredients and top up with water to the MAX line. Blend for 20 to 30 seconds. If required, add more water.

Top Tip: Choose *broccoli* with tight, firm florets and avoid bunches that appear dry and have begun to separate.

Health Benefits

Broccoli is so good for you! It is a great source of vitamins K and C, folate (folic acid) and also provides potassium and fibre. Vitamin C builds collagen, which forms body tissue and bone, and helps cuts and wounds to heal. Vitamin C is a powerful antioxidant and protects the body from damaging free radicals.

Love yourself enough to live a healthy lifestyle.

THANKS FOR READING

We really hope that you have enjoyed the recipes in this book.

If you have found this book useful we would ***really*** appreciate it if you could spare a moment please to leave a review on Amazon.

It really helps and encourages us to keep on creating books. If you have any suggestions or questions please do feel free to get in contact with us at hello@nononsensenosh.com

If you have any smoothie recipe suggestions, we would love to hear from you too!

Happy blending.

Printed in Great Britain
by Amazon

61931666R00077